Truly Foul & Cheesy™
& Cheesy™
Dinosaur
Facts
& Jokes

Published in Great Britain in MMXVIII by
Book House, an imprint of
The Salariya Book Company Ltd
25 Marlborough Place, Brighton BN1 1UB
www.salariya.com

ISBN: 978-1-912006-26-7

S A L A R I Y A

1 3 5 7 9 8 6 4 2

A CIP catalogue record for this book is available
from the British Library.

Printed and bound in China.
Printed on paper from sustainable sources.

Created and designed by
David Salariya.

Visit
www.salariya.com
for our online catalogue and
free fun stuff.

PAPER FROM

SUSTAINABLE
FORESTS

Author:
John Townsend worked as a
secondary school teacher before
becoming a full-time writer.
He specialises in illuminating and
humorous information books for
all ages.

Artist:
David Antram studied at
Eastbourne College of Art and then
worked in advertising for 15 years
before becoming a full-time artist.
He has illustrated many children's
non-fiction books.

Truly Foul & Cheesy™

Dinosaur Facts

& Jokes

This Truly Foul & Cheesy
book belongs to:

....

Written by

John Townsend

Illustrated by

David Antram

BOOK HOUSE
a SALARIYA imprint

Introduction

The jokes in here are even older than me!

Warning – reading this book might not make you LOL (laugh out loud) but it could make you GOL (groan out loud), feel sick out loud or SEL (scream even louder). If you are reading this in a library by a SILENCE sign... get ready to be thrown out!

The author really hasn't made anything up in this book (apart from some daft limericks and jokes).

He checked out the foul facts as best he could and even double-checked the fouler bits to make sure – so please don't get too upset if you find out something different or meet a **REALLY** old scientist/world expert/total genius palaeontologist (fossil expert) or Stegosaurus who happens to know better.

Official Warning

This book isn't JUST about dinosaurs, as the occasional non-dinosaur from prehistoric times might pop up (or even poop up). That's because flying monsters such as pterosaurs weren't technically dinosaurs but were from a separate group of flying reptiles.

In fact, scientists have spent a lot of time working out how flying reptiles pooped. Were they like today's birds, which release their liquid and solid waste at the same time (as one runny, sloppy splat), or did they poop and pee separately, like mammals?

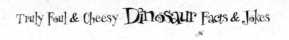

This question may never have bothered you before but if you want to read a foul book like this, such things can't be dodged (particularly if a Pterodactyl happens to be flying over you).

I just had a peep

7

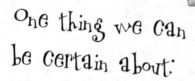

One thing we can be certain about:

Pterodactyls, Pterodaustros and Pteranodons wouldn't have made the slightest sound when they relieved themselves.

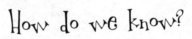

How do we know?

With these **3** creatures the **P** is always silent. (Unlucky, the jokes will get far worse and so will the amount of dinosaur poo). **Y**ou have been warned...

Back to the Prehistoric
(60-200 million years ago)

- Before getting too foul and cheesy, you might like a quick reminder of some of those wow dinosaur facts that never fail to amaze and surprise. Don't forget, that although a few of the 700 or so named dinosaurs were absolute monsters, many of them were relatively small.

- The average size of a dinosaur is thought to be smaller than humans and not much bigger than a sheep – even though they were very different in shape and colour.

- In fact, we can't really know for sure what colours dinosaurs were. We assume they were similar to today's reptile greeny-browns, but why not imagine a stripy Triceratops, a pink-spotted Stegosaurus or even a multi-coloured Massospondylus? If you can imagine all that as well as say it, you must be a genius!

• In fact, how you say some of those dinosaur names can be a bit of a nightmare.
Just how do you say DIPLODOCUS? In the UK, it has long been pronounced
dip-low-**DOKE**-us (like in the next limerick) but the American way is now the most agreed:
dip-**LOD**-er-cus. Yet some say 'dip-low-**DOCK**-us' or even 'digh-**PLOD**-uh-kuss.'
No wonder it's often called just plain DIPPY.

Call me what you like - I can still sit on you.

That thingamy-saw-us:

Limerick

Look closely and make sure you focus
On that beast that could squash us
and choke us.
Watch it slumber and lumber
Like a monster cucumber...
A dirty great green Diplodocus!

Watch out when you start a new chapter,
As a ravenous Velociraptor
Might be lurking within
With a bloodcurdling grin...
To become your carnivorous captor.
Yikes!

11

5 Fast Facts

to start you off –
so you can show off to any
passing dinosaur!

1 Dinosaurs lived on Earth from about 230 million years ago to about 65 million years ago. That's a period of Earth's history called the Mesozoic ('middle life') Era. Dinosaurs lived during all three periods of this era: the Triassic, Jurassic and Cretaceous. That's long before humans appeared.

2 Meat-eating dinosaurs are known as theropods, which means 'beast-footed', because they had sharp, hooked claws on their toes for hunting. In contrast, plant-eating dinosaurs tended to have blunt hooves or toenails.

Dinosaur skulls had large holes or 'windows' that made their skulls lighter. Some of the largest skulls were as long as a car.

 Most meat eaters walked on two feet. This made them faster and left their 'hands' free to grab their prey. Most plant eaters walked on four feet to better carry their massively heavy bodies. Some plant eaters could probably balance on two feet for a short time but they weren't much good at running marathons.

 Some of the biggest plant eaters had to eat almost a tonne of food a day. This is like eating a bus-sized pile of vegetation every single day. And yes, you've guessed... a few munching dinosaurs would dump tonnes of dino dung each day. The Jurassic was more 'Poo-rassic' and not so much prehistoric as poop-horrific!

Dino names

The word 'dinosaur' comes from two Greek words and means terrible lizard. In Greek, deinos means 'terrible' and sauros is the word for 'lizard'. The term was first used in 1842 by Sir Richard Owen in his 'Report on British Fossil Reptiles'. Had he called them 'interesting lizards' we would now be talking about prosagogosaurs!

Owen studied large fossils that looked like lizard bones, but were about the size of giant elephant bones. They were much too large to have come from any modern-day reptiles, so Owen assumed they came from a separate group of ancient animals that had died out long ago.

That seemed like a crazy idea at the time. It was over 60 years later that another fossil hunter discovered the first T. rex remains. This name came from Greek and Latin: Tyrannosaurus rex, which means 'king of the tyrant lizards'.

Palaeontology is the study of fossil records. It is only in the last 150 years or so that scientists have begun to piece together the evidence left by dinosaurs, such as their bones, impressions left in rock and, yes, their fossilised poop. From all this evidence, scientists think some dinosaurs may have lived to be up to 300 years old.

Fossilised dinosaur poo is called coprolite and it can tell scientists a lot about the creatures that left piles of it behind. Some people even wear coprolite as jewellery – so it is possible to polish a poo!

Six
Daft Dinosaurs

1 Sleepyshorus
A dozy dinosaur after a late night

2 Stinkasaurus
A smelly dinosaur on a dung heap

3 Hallelujahchorus
A musical dinosaur

4 Wordythesaurus
A dinosaur that swallowed a dictionary

5 Nowayitsawus
A dinosaur wearing broken glasses

6 Shadysawus
A dinosaur in sunglasses

Dinosaur Men

Some of the first palaeontologists were a bit like dinosaurs themselves. That's because they were so old-fashioned that they didn't allow women to be members of the Geological Society in London. After all, what did women know about fossils? Well, it just so happens a girl from Dorset, UK helped to start off the great 'dinosaur revolution' in the 1800s. Mary Anning was amazing...

Mary Anning

Mary Anning lived in Lyme Regis on the south coast of England – now called the Jurassic Coast because of all the fossils found there. Mary collected fossils and shells to sell, as her family was very poor. She often went fossil hunting after a storm when chunks of cliff fell away – dangerously exposing fossils never seen before.

Hmm – this looks like a squaloraja polyspondyla

Mary taught herself how to read, write and draw, and to understand the way the fossilised animals that she found were formed. She discovered that by grinding up belemnites (squid-like creatures), the mixture could be turned into an ink for writing and drawing. Her sales inspired the famous tongue twister 'she sells sea shells on the seashore'.

When she was 12, Mary's brother saw the fossilised skull of an Ichthyosaur (a large sea predator) so she dug it up and discovered what turned out to be the first complete Ichthyosaur fossil ever found. This was an important discovery because it challenged the way scientists had thought the natural world had developed. In 1823 Mary discovered another huge sea dinosaur fossil, a Plesiosaurus, and in 1828 she discovered a Pterodactyl. No one knew about such creatures from millions of years ago.

Mary Anning

Many scientists came to visit Mary because she knew such a lot about fossils and her discoveries are still on display at the Natural History Museum in London. She died in 1847 without the recognition she deserved – until now. In her lifetime she wasn't taken as seriously as she should have been because she was a woman from a poor background, whereas most scientists were men from wealthy families.

Limerick

Mary Anning found many a fossil
And crowds came to haggle and jostle
To take away bones
And fossilised stones...
But her Ichthyosaur was colossal!

A professor of palaeontology
Owes a ten-year-old girl an apology
For telling her wrongly
That dinos fought strongly...
But otherwise, he's so very knowledgy!
(Although some dinosaurs were
aggressive hunters, many were
peaceful vegetarians.)

DID YOU KNOW?

The word fossil comes from the Latin for 'dug up'. So technically speaking, you eat fossils. Well, chips come from potatoes that are dug up. D'oh! Enjoy your next dollop of mashed fossil.

Extreme Dinosaurs

Even though there is still much to be learned about life on earth **100** million years ago, new discoveries keep revealing some foul, scary and mind-boggling dinosaur secrets.

In fact, just when we think we know the biggest ever dinosaur that lived, someone uncovers the fossilised remains of something even bigger.

Dinosaur experts don't know for certain why some dinosaurs were so huge, but maybe conditions all those millions of years ago, such as climate and food supplies, were just right for some species to reach a whopping great size.

Sauropod dinosaurs

The largest sauropod dinosaurs (four-legged plant-eaters with long necks and tails, but tiny brains) weighed close to 100 tonnes and are often described as 'feats of engineering'. Just how did they get around without falling over and not being able to get up?

Sauropods include the largest land animals ever to have lived, surviving for around 100 million years (about 200-100 million years ago). Fossil footprints show that sauropod dinosaurs travelled in herds, probably very slowly – apart from their tails.

Scientists believe that some sauropods, such as Diplodocus, Apatosaurus (once called brontosaurus) and the record-breaking heavyweight Argentinosaurus, could whip-crack their tails so fast they broke the sound barrier! The tip of their tails could probably crack at 750 miles per hour and sound like a cannon firing. That might even scare off a Tyrannosaurus.

One of the longest sauropod dinosaurs was Seismosaurus, which measured over 40 metres. That's as long as five buses. This 'Quake Lizard' is among the longest land animals ever!

Q: How do you know if there's a
   Seismosaurus under your bed?
A: Because your nose will be squashed on
   the ceiling.

A few other monsters were also munching their
way through the treetops:
Brachiosaurus weighed 80 tonnes, the size of
17 large elephants. It was a good 13 metres tall
and 26 metres long and is the largest dinosaur
skeleton to be displayed in a museum – in
an enormous room as its skull is four storeys
above the ground.

Cheesy Joke Alert

A tourist at a museum was staring up at the huge dinosaur skeleton in awe. She asked the assistant, 'Can you tell me how old these sauropod bones are?'

The guard replied, 'They are one hundred and forty five million, five years and six months old.'

'That's a very precise number,' the tourist said. 'How do you know their age so exactly?'

The assistant answered, 'Well, those bones were one hundred and forty five million years old when I started working here – and that was exactly five years, six months ago.'

I say, I say, I say...

Q: What do you call a dinosaur as tall as a house, with long sharp teeth and 12 claws on each foot?

A: Sir.

Argentinosaurus

Argentinosaurus currently holds the record for being both the heaviest and the longest land animal ever. Despite its huge size, Argentinosaurus laid eggs about the size of a rugby ball, so its young had a lot of growing to do to reach the 37 metre adult size which would probably have taken 40 years or more. It seems Argentinosaurus and its relatives may have lived on in South America longer than other sauropods.

Scientists do not know the exact lifespan of dinosaurs, but they estimate some individuals lived anywhere from 75 to 300 years in total.

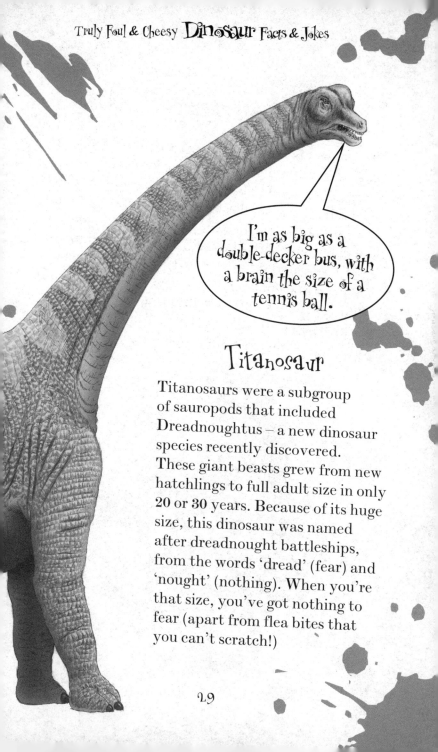

I'm as big as a double-decker bus, with a brain the size of a tennis ball.

Titanosaur

Titanosaurs were a subgroup of sauropods that included Dreadnoughtus – a new dinosaur species recently discovered. These giant beasts grew from new hatchlings to full adult size in only 20 or 30 years. Because of its huge size, this dinosaur was named after dreadnought battleships, from the words 'dread' (fear) and 'nought' (nothing). When you're that size, you've got nothing to fear (apart from flea bites that you can't scratch!)

29

More eggs-eptional finds

All dinosaurs laid eggs. About 40 kinds of dinosaur eggs have been discovered of various shapes and sizes. Many tend to be about the size and shape of a rugby ball. The smallest dinosaur egg so far found is only 3 cm long. Once the egg has been fossilised it will become hard like rock. The largest dinosaur eggs discovered so far were in China in the 1990s. They were 60 cm long. Other eggs have been found of different sizes buried in different parts of the world. They were all past their sell-by date and wouldn't be much good for making an omelette.

I'm only tiny and I've got hollow bones.

Smallest dinosaurs

No – not the titchysaurus! The smallest fully-grown fossil dinosaur is the little bird-hipped plant-eater Lesothosaurus, which was only the size of a chicken. The Compsognathus ('pretty jaw') was 1 metre long and probably weighed just 2.5 kg.

FIVE FOULISH FACTS

1 Snakes and lizards shed their skin when they grow. Researchers believe that dinosaurs may have done the same. That would mean piles of crusty old skin scales would be rotting all over the place. Yuck!

2 Dinosaurs often swallowed large rocks. These rocks stayed in their stomach and helped grind up food. Crocodiles today do the same.

3 Plant-eating dinosaurs were probably the first culprits to affect climate change. All the gas from giant dino-farts would have contributed to early global warming.

4 Modern birds and reptiles have a single body opening for expelling urine and poop. Palaeontologists believe that dinosaurs' bottoms were similarly designed. (Maybe they examined a tricerabottom instead of a Triceratops... tee hee!)

5 Palaeontologists don't always get things right. Piecing together all those broken fossil bones can be very tricky. When Gideon Mantell (1790–1852) was putting together an Iguanodon's skeleton, he put its thumb claw on top of its nose. It stayed that way for 40 years. Edward Cope (1840–1897) reconstructed Elasmosaurus ('thin plate') with its head on the end of its tail. Oops! Apatosaurus (Brontosaurus) once appeared in museums with the head of a completely different dinosaur; Camarasaurus ('chambered lizard'). Doh.

Dinosaur Riddles

(because they're so ancient)

Q: What do you call a dinosaur with foul language?
A: Bronto-swore-us.

Q: What do you call a dinosaur with a refrigerator?
A: Bronto-store-ice.

Q: What do you call a dinosaur in high heels?
A: Feet-are-sore-us

Q: What do you call a dinosaur playing hide and seek?
A: Do-you-think-he-saw-us?

Q: What do you call a dinosaur that's a noisy sleeper?
A: Bronto-snorus.

Fifteen Fabulous, Fascinating Favourite, Formidable, Frightful Facts

WARNING – TRICKY NAMES COMING UP

1 Measuring about 17 metres long, Liopleurodon was the biggest ocean reptile, but only half the size of a blue whale, whose body is bigger than any dinosaur at 33 metres.

2 Most meat-eating dinosaurs had bones filled with air. Though their bones were huge, they weren't as heavy as they looked. Birds have the same kind of hollow bones which keep them super-light for flying.

3 Some dinosaurs had feet like a rhinoceros, elephant, bird or a pig. The biggest footprints ever found were a metre across and over a metre long.

36

4 Plant-eating dinosaurs often lived together for protection, like herding animals do today. Herds ranged from a few adults and their young to thousands of animals.

Deinosuchus was a huge prehistoric crocodile. It most likely had the strongest bite of any dinosaur, including Tyrannosaurus rex. It weighed eight times as much as today's crocodiles.

6 Sauropods ('Lizard-Footed') could travel many miles a day on their huge legs. Their fossilised trackways or 'superhighways' can still be seen today.

Unlike sauropods, two-legged dinosaurs (the hunting carnivores) were usually faster on their feet than their larger four-legged vegetarian cousins. Although their average walking speed was probably about 5 kilometres (3 miles) per hour, peak running speeds varied from about 30 to 80 km/h (20 to 50 mph).

 Corythosaurus had a big, hollow crest connected to its nose. The crest worked like an echo chamber, letting it make a loud blast of noise. Scary!

 Struthiomimus ('ostrich mimic') made high-pitched, screechy noises similar to an ostrich. It was a noisy world back then.

10 The toothiest dinosaur was the duck-billed Hadrosaur ('bulky lizard'). It could have over 1,000 tiny teeth and it continually grew new ones – ideal for chomping on tough pine cones.

I spend most of my time at the dentist.

The dinosaur with the thickest skull was the Pachycephalosaurus. Its skull grew up to 20 cm thick. (Yes, it was thick in the head.)

 Parasaurolophus had a crest that looked like half of a trombone. The male's crest was almost 2 metres long, which was the biggest out of all the dinosaurs.

Yikes - all these scary names!

 The dinosaur with the longest claws was the Therizinosaurus ('reaping lizard'). Its claws were up to a metre long – for stripping bark from trees or lashing out at predators. Useful advice: never upset a Therizinosaurus.

Generally, if a dinosaur stood on all four feet, it was a solid vegetarian. Even so, it would probably stand on anyone who annoyed it.

If none of these facts are foul enough for you, try this one about vile vomit. Fossilised dinosaur sick was found in Italy and experts have been studying 'gastric pellets' once coughed up by a dinosaur. The dollop of prehistoric sick contained undigested lizard bones. In 2015 a team of researchers published their findings. Nice work!

Six Cheesy Riddles

Q: When can three giant dinosaurs get under an umbrella and not get wet?
A: When it's not raining.

These are too cheesy even for me.

Q: What is big, yellow and prickly, has three eyes and eats rocks?
A: A big, yellow, prickly three-eyed rock eater.

44

Q: What's as big as a dinosaur but weighs nothing?
A: Its shadow.

Q: What's yellow and dangerous?
A: Dinosaur-infested custard.

Q: Why did the dinosaur paint its feet yellow?
A: So it could hide upside-down in the custard.

Q: How would you feel if you saw a dinosaur in your backyard?
A: Very old.

10 Dinosaurs (or 'almost dinosaurs') you wouldn't want in your bedroom

1 The fearsome Tyrannosaurus Rex

You'd need to hide under your bed if this top predator ever barged into your bedroom. Tyrannosaurus rex (or T. rex) ruled North America 68–65 million years ago. Its massive skull measured 1.5 metres and was balanced at the other end by a long heavy tail. The jaw, filled with huge saw-edged teeth (some almost 30 cm long), could rip other dinosaurs apart. As top predator and mighty scavenger, this 'tyrant lizard king' was one of the scariest at over 12 metres long and 4 metres tall.

Q: What do you give a T. rex with a cold?

A: Plenty of room. Why? It could sneeze buckets of snot. Scientists have calculated that the large sinuses of a T. rex (the cavities behind the nose and cheek bones where mucus is produced) could hold about 30 litres of slimy, sticky, squelchy, sloppy, slippery snot. One big sneeze and... run for it!

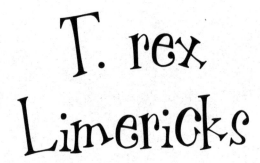

T. rex Limericks

If you see a T. rex start to shiver
And its nostrils go all of a quiver,
Then you'd better run fast
As a snotty-fuelled blast
Will spew like a slobbery river.

We once met a Tyrannosaurus
But sadly it didn't ignore us.
It opened its jaws
With such ear-splitting roars
So we prayed, sang a hymn and a
Chorus (then legged it).

Tyrannosaurus rex ate up to 20 tonnes of meat a year. Some scientists believe it may have been able to run as fast as 18 mph, but other scientists believe it couldn't run because it was so big. Even so, its huge back legs and tiny front legs (not much longer than human arms) could be lethal if you got in the way.

Giant fleas were a big problem for many dinosaurs and a probable killer of smaller species. These insects could reach 2 or 3 cm long and had strong mouthparts for piercing dinosaur scales.

Other parasites also infested T. rex jaws. Being cannibals and preying on smaller dinosaurs, T. rex would catch even more parasites from prey and probably got smothered in itches that it couldn't scratch with its short arms. An itchy, irritable T. rex with a temper would definitely be something to avoid. So would its scary bigger relatives. If you let any into your bedroom, you've only got yourself to blame.

Ahhh

One of the biggest hunters was the Spinosaurus ('spine lizard') which could reach 15 metres long and weigh 3 times more than a T. rex. You really wouldn't want to meet one.

There was also the formidable Allosaurus ('different lizard')

Allosaurus had a lot of sharp teeth – some up to 10 cm long. They shed their teeth frequently and scientists have found a lot of them. These hunters were 9 to 12 metres long and chunky – easily able to gang up in packs against other dinosaurs.

Another of the biggest predator dinosaurs ever discovered was bigger than T. rex but slightly smaller than the Spinosaurus. It was the suitably named Giganotosaurus. Despite its size, it had a tiny brain – the size of a small cucumber.

Limerick

A Tyrannosaurus rex winked
At a Giganotosaurus that blinked
And whispered, 'You're clever,
And I'll love you forever...'
'Forget it, mate – we'll soon be extinct.'

2 Stegosaurus

The Stegosaurus had the smallest brain for its body size of any known dinosaur. Its body was the size of a van, but its brain was the size of a walnut so it probably wasn't too clever. It's a bit like your brain being the size of a pea, so it was hopeless at maths.

A Stegosaurus had huge plates sticking up from its back. Although scientists aren't really sure what the plates were for, they may have helped the Stegosaurus control its body temperature by regulating blood flow through them. A Stegosaurus may also have been able to control its skin colour this way, to attract a mate or scare predators.

6
RANDOM
Stegosaurus facts

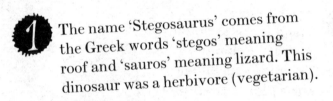 The name 'Stegosaurus' comes from the Greek words 'stegos' meaning roof and 'sauros' meaning lizard. This dinosaur was a herbivore (vegetarian).

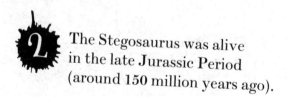 The Stegosaurus was alive in the late Jurassic Period (around 150 million years ago).

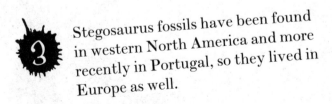 Stegosaurus fossils have been found in western North America and more recently in Portugal, so they lived in Europe as well.

4 A fully grown Stegosaurus was around 9 metres in length, 4 metres in height and up to nearly 5 tonnes in weight. It could probably only move up to 8 kilometres per hour.

5 The Stegosaurus had tail spikes that reached almost a metre long.

6 The first ever Stegosaurus skeleton was found in Colorado, USA. Colorado's nickname is the Stegosaurus State.

Q: What has a spiked tail, plates on its back and sixteen wheels?
A: A Stegosaurus on roller skates.

Limerick

Which dinosaur was surely
the lumpiest?
A Stegosaurus could well be
the bumpiest,
As well as quite stumpy
And terribly humpy...
Or the dumpiest, grumpiest,
frumpiest!

Why wouldn't a T.rex
ever harm a Stegosaurus?

Troodon

3 Compared with a Stegosaurus, a Troodon
('tooth that wounds') was a genius.
It had a brain the size of a mammal's
today so it was a brainy hunting
dinosaur, about 2 metres long. It also had
grasping hands and stereoscopic vision
so it was smart, feathery and dangerous.
You could fit a few in your bedroom but
they'd be tricky to house-train.

Q: Why did the Troodon cover itself in
vegetable stock and cream of mushrooms?
A: So it could hide in the primeval soup.*

*primeval soup was a theory of where the
first life on earth began – in a bubbling
mixture of chemicals and cells. (It was
also probably very lumpy, smelly and
tasted disgusting...)

Because they
weren't both around at
the same time.

 Triceratops

Triceratops, with its three horns and bony frill around the back of its head was 3 metres in height and 9 metres long. This dinosaur, with a top speed of 25 km/h, used its horns and frill in fights against its main predator, Tyrannosaurs. Although a vegetarian, Triceratops could be a fierce fighter. Palaeontologists have uncovered horn and skull Triceratops bones with healed-up Tyrannosaur tooth marks, suggesting the Triceratops successfully fended off its vicious attacker.

Humans' eyes face forward so that they can see in 3D. Plant-eating dinosaurs, like the Triceratops, had eyes looking out to each side, so they could watch for danger while they fed. It had the biggest skull of any dinosaur – up to 2 metres long, with a bony shield over its neck. They're probably not very cuddly at bedtime.

More Cheesiness

Q: What is large and has a frill, horns and four wheels?
A: A Triceratops on a skateboard.

Q: What do you get if you cross a Triceratops with high explosives?
A: Dino-mite.

Q: How do you stop a Triceratops from smelling?
A: Put a peg on its nose.

5 Iguanodon

Plant-eating Iguanodons were large dinosaurs that could walk on two legs or on all four. They had large five-fingered hands with a spiked thumb, three middle fingers and a grasping fifth finger. Herds of Iguanodons lived in Europe (including the Isle of White in England) and North America.

Iguanodons were big and bulky – growing to about 12 metres long. Because they were so heavy they could only run as fast as about 14 miles per hour.

Q: How can you tell if an Iguanodon is in your bedroom?
A: Firstly, the door won't close. Secondly, all the walls have gone.

Q: What should you do if you find an Iguanodon in your bed?
A: Sleep somewhere else.

Iguanodons disappeared about 120 million years ago - like rats leaving a sinking ship.

⑥ Velociraptor

Velociraptors had very powerful back legs with long claws that could rip into their prey (and make a real mess of your bedroom). They were fierce hunters and would probably hunt together in packs. No small dinosaur would have been able to escape from their attack. It's just as well a Velociraptor was not as big as a T. rex.

Velociraptors were only about 1.8 metres long, very fast, agile and most likely covered in feathers. How would you like one for a pet? You'd be wise not to let it indoors.

Q: What type of Velociraptor
   can jump higher than a tree?
A: Any type – as a tree can't
   jump. Doh.

7

Archaeopteryx

Is it a bird? Is it a dinosaur? Well, it's a sort of birdosaur-dinobird.

Swoop

The Archaeopteryx is often regarded as the first true bird, with feathers and a beak. Even so, it also had claws on each wing and sharp teeth, making it more like a dinosaur.

It probably lived in trees and glided for short distances, rather than actually flying far. The Archaeopteryx was probably quite intelligent, with a large brain in comparison to its body size.

Newborn birds took around 3 years to grow to full size – but that wasn't very big. They were only about the size of pigeons, so you could get plenty in your bedroom... worth a try? The Archaeopteryx ate bugs, frogs and lizards and may have caught smaller creatures in its wings.

Q: Why did the Archaeopteryx catch the worm?
A: Because it was an early bird. In fact, it was the earliest!

8 Sarcosuchus

This scary cousin of the dinosaurs was a super-croc and doubtless gobbled up dinosaurs that went down to the river for a drink.

Sarcosuchus was one of the biggest crocodiles ever to live as some reached about 12 metres long. It lived just over 100 million years ago in Africa and South America and was almost twice as long and heavy as its modern relative, the saltwater crocodile. The power of its bite would have been stronger than most other creatures, apart from a T. rex.

A fully-grown Sarcosuchus would have been capable of breaking the neck of a large dinosaur, so never let one into your bedroom unsupervised.

Q: What smells fouler and roars louder than a Sarcosuchus, and is very hard to say?
A: Two Sarcosuchuses!

A Sarcosuchus Limerick

Have you heard of that huge
crocodilian,
That truly enormous reptilian?
The super Sarcosuchus
Dribbled thick yucky goo-mucus
As it chomped dinosaurs by the
gazillion.
Yikes!

69

9 Pterodactyl
(pronounced: ter-u-dak-til)

Pterodactyl is the term for winged reptiles (not technically dinosaurs), usually called pterosaurs (with 130 or so different types). These creatures had a wingspan of anywhere between several centimetres to well over 10 metres. They could glide long distances and were carnivores. Perhaps the most terrifying was the Quetzalcoatlus ('KWET-zal-koh-AT-lus') with a wingspan of up to 12 metres.

Quetzalcoatlus was the largest pterosaur that ever lived; in fact, this airplane-sized reptile of North America was the largest animal ever to take to the skies. With a single leap off a cliff, one of these giants would soar through the air, with only a few flaps of its wings. They could likely travel nonstop for anywhere up to 10,000 miles on the lookout for prey to swoop down on and rip apart – so keep your bedroom window closed just in case.

Q: How do you know a Pterodactyl has been in your bedroom?
A: Massive peck marks on your pillow.

Q: Why did the Quetzalcoatlus paint her toenails bright red?
A: So she could hide upside down in the strawberry patch.

10 Plesiosaur

Plesiosaurs were swimming reptiles, rather than true dinosaurs, but they lived alongside them from 220 million years ago until 65 million years ago, when they became extinct at the same time. Their remains have been found all around the world.

Plesiosaurs were long-necked reptiles of the sea, with a swimming speed of about 5 miles per hour. That's not very fast for catching fish so they would have hunted slower, bigger prey.

A Plesiosaur had a broad body, four large flippers and a relatively short tail – a bit like 'a snake strung through a turtle'. The smallest were about 2 metres but the largest were an enormous 20 metres. You'd need a very big fish tank in your bedroom to keep one of those.

Q: How do you know a Plesiosaur has been in your bedroom?
A: There's a large damp patch on the duvet – and a loud trickling noise.
(Unlike a Pterodactyl, there's no silent pee!)

Q: What do you call a very polite swimming reptile that wants to delight you?
A: A pleaseyouosaur.

Look out for the famous Plesiosaur on page 102!

74

Have you heard this tale about the Plesiosaur? It's longer than you think. (Tale, tail – get it?)

A very snooty man was walking round the museum when he stopped beside the skeleton of a Plesiosaur. He peered over at a frame hanging on the wall.
'I suppose this is what the hideous beast was supposed to look like,' he said pompously. 'Such a horrible picture of an ugly monster is what you call an artist's impression, is it?'
'No sir,' replied the assistant. 'That's what we call a mirror.'

What's in a name?

One of the scariest things about dinosaurs is their names. Some of them look like an explosion in a scrabble factory. Just why do so many dinosaurs have such weird names that you can't pronounce without losing your teeth? It's because the palaeontologists who first discovered them often wanted to show off by using a mixture of Greek, Latin and sometimes their own name as well. So rather than a simple descriptive name (like a foulandcheesysaurus), we get such names as (brace yourself for the longest dinosaur name which has 23 letters) Micropachycephalosaurus.

This is pronounced **MY**-cro-**PACK**-ee-**SEFF**-ah-low-**SORE**-us and is Greek for 'tiny thick-headed lizard' (which is quite a good name to call someone who annoys you). Despite such a long name, this dinosaur was under a metre long.

SIX
Silly Names

1 What do you call a dinosaur discovered by Chinese workers at a gas company? No, this isn't a joke. Gasosaurus was like a smaller version of an Allosaurus (a fearsome hunter like a T. rex). Although Gasosaurus might sound as though it had a problem with bottom gas, there is no evidence it had flatulence – otherwise it would have been called a fartasaurus!

It smells like a stinkasaurus in here.

Weirdly, in 2014 a Gasosaurus was the subject of an internet hoax. Someone claimed that a 200-million-year-old Gasosaurus egg stored next to a museum boiler managed to incubate and hatch. Now that really would be interesting!

 You might think a dinosaur called Drinker used to stagger around the swamps of northern Africa looking for beer. Not so. This smallish two-legged plant-eating dinosaur was named after a famous palaeontologist called Edward Drinker Cope.

 Being as long as a couple of cars and weighing as much as a couple of plump hippos, one dinosaur has to put up with the name Irritator. There's no proof it was more irritating than any other theropod (that's a top predator dinosaur on two legs). The reason Irritator was given this name was because when it was discovered by palaeontologists, they were really irritated to find its skull had been deliberately altered by fossil hunters. Ah well, at least it didn't end up as a 'howveryannoyingasaurus'.

Another dinosaur looking like a mini T. rex has the unpronounceable name (unless you say Pee-at-nits-kee-sore-us) Piatnitzkysaurus. It was named after a palaeontologist with an even trickier name. Take a deep breath and hold on to your hat... Alejandro Matveievich Piatnitzky. Why can't all palaeontologists be called Jones?

These jokes are pre-hysterical

Try this for a monstrous name for a dinosaur... Titanophoneus. It actually means 'giant murderer'. So what kind of mighty beast springs to mind? In fact, it was no larger than a big dog so whoever named this dinosaur was guilty of mega exaggeration.

If you've seen the Disney cartoon of Bambi about a cute baby deer, you might be surprised to know a dinosaur was named after it. Bambiraptor was a fierce, deer-sized raptor. A 14 year-old boy stumbled on a Bambiraptor skeleton in 1995 in Montana's Glacier National Park. If it had a long nose, maybe he'd have gone for another Disney cartoon and called it a Pinocchioraptor.

How to become

EXTINCT

without really trying

The big question that has puzzled scientists for over 150 years is 'why did the dinosaurs die out?' There were many ideas about the 'great extinction', but only a few really make sense today. Something happened about 65 million years ago that killed off many of the creatures on the land and in the sea. Either disease or loss of food supply must have caused a major catastrophe.

Fossil evidence shows there was a gradual decline in the dinosaur population 65.5 million years ago, most likely due to large scale climate change. Possibly huge volcanoes threw out enormous quantities of lava, volcanic ash and poisonous gas which darkened the planet.

At about the same time a large asteroid struck the Earth, forming a 112 miles wide crater in what is now the Yucatan Peninsula in Mexico. It would have hit Earth's crust with immense force, sending shockwaves around the world. This impact would have caused extremely cold months or years because of dust in the atmosphere. Plants and gradually the whole food chain would have been affected – from plant-eating dinosaurs to the meat-eating dinosaurs that fed on them.

No land dinosaur much larger than a pig survived, yet some fish, scorpions, birds, insects, snakes, turtles, lizards and crocodiles did survive. Many of their descendants are still with us.

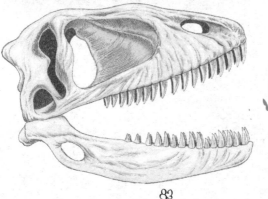

Riddle

Q: How did dinosaurs pass
their final exams?
A: With extinction
(that's dino-speak for 'distinction')

Distinction in extinction

Ever since the dinosaurs disappeared,
other large creatures have come and gone.
Reptiles, mammals and fish that lived after
the dinosaurs have since died out because of
either habitat change or from being hunted
by early humans.

Monsters AFTER the dinosaurs

Titanoboa

- Titanoboa was a monster among prehistoric snakes, about the size and weight of an extremely long school bus (but you wouldn't want to take a ride on it). It could happily gulp you down like a biscuit snack.

- After the dinosaurs were wiped out, it took a few million years for life on earth to get itself together. Titanoboa (along with all sorts of large prehistoric turtles and crocodiles) was one of the first super-sized reptiles to claim a top-of-the-food-chain position.

South America eventually recovered from the plunging global temperatures after the Yucatan meteor impact. After all that dust settled, which obscured the sun and closed down the dinosaurs, modern-day Peru and Colombia warmed up to become tropical. Reptiles like Titanoboa could grow to scary sizes in such conditions – until climates cooled once more and more extinction followed.

Megalodon

The Megalodon super-fish was the largest shark that ever lived, believed to have been 15 to over 21 metres long – the size of three great white sharks! It was as heavy as 16 African bull elephants and a massive prehistoric predator. It is thought Megalodon lived from 23 million years ago to about 2½ million years ago.

•The word 'Megalodon' comes from two Greek words – megas, meaning 'big', and odont, meaning 'tooth'. The Megalodon had five rows of over 270 sharp teeth that could grow over 18 centimetres long. Only T. rex and the sabre-toothed cats are known to have had larger teeth. The Smilodon's fangs (sometimes called a sabre-tooth tiger that lived from about 2½ million years ago to 10,000 years ago) grew up to 28 centimetres. They were used to bite and slash prey.

•Like many other prehistoric giant animals that became extinct, the Megalodon vanished as well (even though some people say they could still be out there!). The cooling of the world's oceans during ice ages probably finished them off forever. Climate change is nothing new and it usually had drastic effects on even the toughest of predators.

•Today's threat to our planet is still from changing climates. Already many animal species have been lost because of damaged habitats. If we don't act fast to save many of today's endangered species, they, too, will become extinct and join the dinosaurs in belonging to a long-lost world.

It used to smell in here but now it's ex-stinked

Woolly Mammoth Poop May Solve Extinction Mystery

What caused the woolly mammoth to become extinct has always been a mystery. But around 10,000 years ago, just as humans were starting to learn about farming, woolly mammoth numbers began to shrink. Did people really hunt them too much or was there another reason why woolly mammoths completely disappeared from mainland habitats and lived only on islands? One herd survived in present-day Alaska until about 4,000 years ago.

Scientists have been studying ancient mammoth dung which, before 10,000 years ago in the arctic plains, was full of the remains of a particular flower. In other words, mammoths chomped away on little flowers called forbs that were full of protein. When these plants disappeared about 10,000 years ago, maybe the mammoths disappeared too. However, the death of the mammoths may have caused the death of the forbs (that relied on mammoth dung compost), so it's still uncertain as to what happened first.

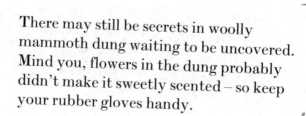

There may still be secrets in woolly mammoth dung waiting to be uncovered. Mind you, flowers in the dung probably didn't make it sweetly scented – so keep your rubber gloves handy.

6 silly
woolly mammoth riddles

Q: What has 5 legs, 3 ears, 2 trunks and 3 tusks?
A: A great woolly mammoth with spare parts.

Q: How do you run over a woolly mammoth?
A: Climb up its tail, run to its head and slide down its trunk.

Q: What do you get if you cross a woolly mammoth and a kangaroo?
A: Big holes all over the ice.

Q: What would you give to a mammoth that is having an anxiety attack?
A: Trunkquilizers

Q: What's the difference between an injured mammoth and a storm?
A: One roars with pain and the other pours with rain.

Q: What is huge, shaggy, has 16 feet and sounds terrible?
A: A mammoth barbershop quartet.

LIVING DINOSAURS TODAY...

maybe

The author who wrote the Sherlock Holmes detective stories was Arthur Conan Doyle and in 1912 he wrote a novel called The Lost World. His story is set in a remote jungle where dinosaurs still survive in modern times. People loved imagining what it must be like to live alongside dinosaurs.

In 1990 another author, Michael Crichton, wrote a story where a dinosaur theme park was the setting. Jurassic Park was a great success, as well as the films that followed. People can't seem to get enough of modern dinosaur adventures... where a T. rex happily gobbles up humans like sweets.

95

Dino-fish

Fossils from a prehistoric fish the size of a human were studied by palaeontologists, who called it a Coelacanth (pronounced SEEL-uh-kanth). It was an enormous, bottom-dwelling fish that lived about 350 million years ago.

It was assumed to be extinct until a live one was caught in 1938 off the coast of South Africa. The second living example of Coelacanth was discovered in an Indonesian market in 1997, and a live specimen was caught one year later.

Are you calling me a living dinosaur? How dare you!

You wouldn't want to eat one, though. Its flesh has high amounts of oil and wax that make it taste foul and can make you ill. They're also slimy, their thick scales ooze mucus and their bodies are full of oily gunge.

But being so gross has helped them survive for millions of years. So if Coelacanths have remained virtually unseen all that time, maybe other prehistoric creatures may still be out there. Is it possible a few dinosaurs are still hiding in remote parts of the world? What if....

97

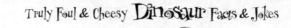

Living Pterosaurs

For years people have reported seeing large creatures swooping across the sky. Now and again there are claims that real live pterosaurs are on the loose. In 2015 a video taken in Boise, Idaho, showed what looked like a pterosaur soaring across the sky.

The creature appears to have the telltale signs of a pterosaur; a massive bat-like wingspan and a large backward-pointing crest. Could it be real? Was it a hoax, a glider or maybe a kite? Opinions remain divided.

There have been many other pterosaur 'sightings' around the world. Texas and California have had various reported sightings, some by the police. In Texas, there were reports of pterosaurs in Harlingen in 1976, San Antonio in 1976 and Los Fresnos in 1982. No photos were taken but large three-toed tracks were found.

Could some of the vast swampy areas in the thick forests of Zambia in Africa also be home to living pterosaurs? According to some people, a creature known as Kongamato (which means 'the breaker of boats') has attacked fishermen on rivers and lakes. Or maybe people have just seen large shoebill storks which have a wingspan of 2 metres.

Maybe it's just a matter of time before someone somewhere finds real proof... or not.

Lake Monsters

Hundreds of lakes around the world are said to hide monsters in their murky depths – from Scotland's Loch Ness to Canada's Lake Okanagan, America's Lake Champlain to Argentina's Lake Nahuel.

For over 1000 years, the mystery deep in Loch Ness has brought monster hunters to find 'Nessie'. After a road was made around the loch, more and more people reported seeing the 'plesiosaur' raising its head above the misty water. Some people have taken hoax photographs to keep the monster story alive.

Believers and researchers ask what creature could be so big – a submarine-size shape moving through the water. A plesiosaur dinosaur seems the most popular explanation, even though no one has ever been able to produce convincing proof for the existence of this world famous 'beastie'. Unless, of course, it really was a secret submarine.

Loch Limerick

If you swim in the loch,
don't get stressy
If the water churns frothy
and messy
Just flee back to shore
From the Plesiosaur...
That infamous Scot known
as Nessie.

I'm itching to tell you more Nessie jokes

Cheesy Nessie Jokes

Q: What is large, yellow, lives in Scotland and has never been seen?

A: The Loch Ness Canary.

Q: What is cold, stripy, lives in Scotland and is often seen and heard in the glens?

A: The Loch Ness Ice Cream Van.

Q: What is large, scaly and humpy, lives in Scotland and has a massive trunk?

A: The Loch Ness Monster going on holiday.

Did you hear about the man who tried to cross the Loch Ness Monster with a sheep? He had to get a new sheep.

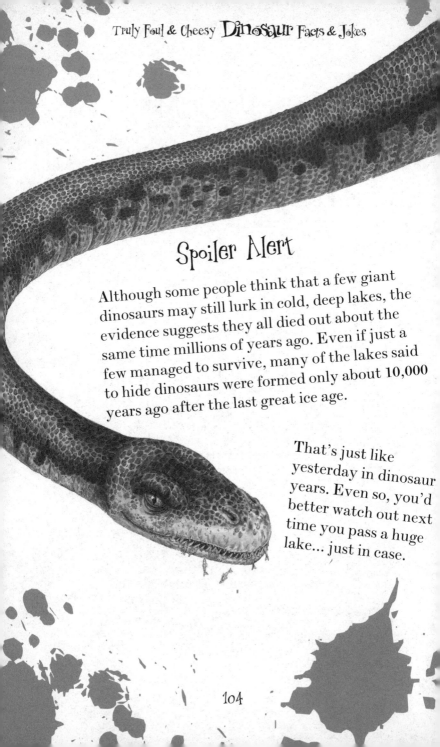

Spoiler Alert

Although some people think that a few giant dinosaurs may still lurk in cold, deep lakes, the evidence suggests they all died out about the same time millions of years ago. Even if just a few managed to survive, many of the lakes said to hide dinosaurs were formed only about 10,000 years ago after the last great ice age.

That's just like yesterday in dinosaur years. Even so, you'd better watch out next time you pass a huge lake... just in case.

A Living Sauropod... possibly

In the remote jungles of central Africa and the Likouala Swamp of The Congo, stories have been told for 200 years of a dinosaur-like creature said to be 12 metres long, with brownish-grey skin and a long, bendy neck. Many believe that it lives in caves it digs in riverbanks, attacking elephants, hippos and crocodiles by thrashing its tail, even though it is a strict vegetarian. Local tribes call the creature Mokele-Mbembe, which means 'the beast that stops the river'.

Strange noises and footprints in the forest and only a few fuzzy photos are so far all that has been found by scientists. A Chicago biologist who took two expeditions in search of the Mokele-Mbembe believes that the descriptions of the creature suggest 'a small sauropod dinosaur' but there is no firm evidence, other than stories and the frightened faces of local fishermen. What do you think?

105

A FINAL

dip into dino dung

Some people collect stamps, others collect works of art and some people collect poop (well, coprolite or fossilised dino dung). In the 2017 edition of the Guinness Book of Records, you will find that George Frandsen (USA) has the world's largest collection of coprolite, otherwise known as fossilised faeces. He has piled up an amazing 1,277 pieces of prehistoric poo since he began his collection as a palaeontology student.

He collected poop from 15 states in the USA and 8 countries worldwide.

A prize piece is 'Precious', his largest coprolite, weighing in at a whopping 1.92 kg. You'll be pleased to learn that coprolites are as hard as a rock and they have no smell.

George's advice for anyone looking to set a world record is: 'Have lots of passion for whatever you're doing. Mine is coprolite – fossilised faeces ... whatever your passion you should follow it.' That's great advice – and not to be sniffed at.

And in case you were wondering, one of the longest fossilised dinosaur poops on record is over a metre long and it was sold at auction (maybe it was bought by a poo-seum!)

GROSS ALERT

Have YOU drunk dinosaur urine? (Almost certainly)

According to some scientists, every glass of water today contains liquid from Jurassic times. Yes, you've guessed it...the next time you reach for a glass of water, you could be about to sip on dinosaur pee.

Apparently, the amount of water on the Earth has remained about the same for millions of years. Around 121,000 cubic miles of water falls on the Earth in the form of rain and snow every year, as it keeps moving around the planet in the water cycle.

Experts tell us that most of the water molecules have never been drunk by another human, but almost every single one has been previously drunk by a dinosaur. This means that in every glass of water you drink, there's a lot of water which has already passed through a dinosaur and come out the other end. Mmmmm.

OOPS!

Even experts make
dino-bloopers
Meet the Bloopersauruses...

When dinosaurs were first discovered in the 1800s, naturalists were baffled by the idea of elephant-sized lizards with bird-sized brains. Some believed a Stegosaurus must have had a second brain in its rear end in a kind of hollow in its rump.

In 1868, the American palaeontologist Edward Drinker Cope pieced together the skeleton of a dinosaur but, like doing a jigsaw without a picture to follow, he had to make some guesses. He ended up sticking the head on the wrong end – on the tail instead of the neck. Oops. It was more like a backtofrontasaurus!

Eventually the world learned that no dinosaur had two brains. The cavity in the Stegosaurus's tail was probably for storing energy in the form of glycogen. The original theory was a no-brainer!

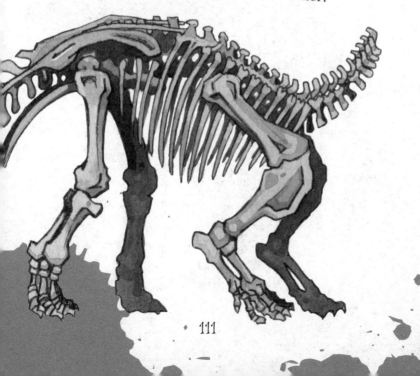

The UK's most famous dinosaur moves after 112 years!

Dippy the Diplodocus, who famously stood in the entrance hall of London's Natural History Museum since 1905 began to stir in 2017...

The 21-metre long dino began travelling around the UK to let more people see him (with a little help from museum staff). He had to be flat-packed and put back together piece by piece. In fact, Dippy looks like a real Diplodocus skeleton, but he's actually a plaster model. Taking Dippy's place in the museum now is a blue whale skeleton – but unlike Dippy, this one is the real deal. The weighty whale is a heavy haul of bones at nearly 4.5 tonnes (we know that because she went by train to the whale-weigh station, tee hee).

After his tour, Dippy's new home is the museum gardens, with him re-cast in bronze. If he gets rained on, it doesn't matter – he just becomes Drippy Dippy (until he's bone dry again).

A Dippy Limerick

On the banks of the great
Mississippi
Where the water flows
choppy and nippy,
A very precocious
Unclothed Diplodocus (stripped
to the bone)
Dives in and screams,
"I'm Skinny Dippy!"

BIG
dinosaur
skeletons make
BIGGER
MONEY

Just in case you want to buy your own dinosaur, you'd better start saving. Bones and skeletons sell for huge money today. Over 20 years ago, one of the world's most famous fossils fetched a big price but it would be far more today. Sue, a T. rex skeleton, was sold to a Chicago museum for $8.3 million in 1997. So it may be better to buy it in a sale when prices are cut to the bone!

And Finally...

Here's a final mind-boggling thought for you to sleep on. Although the Earth is extraordinarily ancient, imagine it as a house that's just 200 years old. Different lodgers have lived there down the years and some lie buried in the garden (just like the dinosaurs). Today new visitors have moved in – in the very last minute. That's just how it is with the arrival of humans on our planet. We've only lived on Earth for a tiny amount of its history and we don't know how long we'll stay. Will we last as long as the dinosaurs did?

We've only just got here and hardly had a chance to uncover all the Earth's secrets yet. It's only a matter of time. And will dinosaurs ever return? Don't have too many nightmares!

QUIZ

1. When did dinosaurs become extinct?

a) 65 million years ago

b) 150 million years ago

c) Last Tuesday

2. What is a theropod?

a) A flying dinosaur

b) A two-legged, meat-eating dinosaur

c) A portable music device

3. What is Coprolite?

a) A type of insect

b) A sugar-free soft drink

c) Fossilised poo

4. What is a sauropod?

a) A four-legged, long-necked dinosaur

b) A two-legged, sharp-clawed dinosaur

c) A dinosaur that has bumped its head

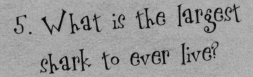

5. What is the largest shark to ever live?

a) Jaws

b) Great White

c) Megalodon

6. What type of dinosaur stood in the London Natural History museum entrance hall?

a) Tyrannosaurus rex

b) Diplodocus

c) A stuffed Victorian palaeontologist

7. What was a Plesiosaur?

a) A large, swimming reptile

b) A leisure centre

c) A species of carnivorous dinosaur

8. What did a stegosaurus have on its tail?

a) Spots

b) Fur

c) Spikes

9. Which dinosaur had the longest claws?

a) Therizinosaurus

b) Scratchandmakeyousoreus

c) Tyrannosaurus rex

10. Which dinosaur had a wingspan of up to 12 metres?

a) Quizletcoatlus

b) Quetzalcoatlus

c) Quackquackcoatlus

GLOSSARY

Asteroid: small planet-shaped bodies of ice and rock that orbit our solar system and sometimes collide with the Earth.

Climate: the qualities of the atmosphere in a particular environment over a period of time, such as the temperature, humidity, amount of rain and weather patterns.

Fossil: the remains of a living organism that lived thousands of millions of years ago, preserved in the Earth's crust.

Ichthyosaur: a group of species of extinct water-dwelling reptiles.

Lava: extremely hot liquid rock that erupts from volcanoes.

Palaeontology: the study of fossils to try to understand the biology of ancient and long-vanished life forms from the distant past.

Prehistoric: the period before written records of history began, from the dawn of life on Earth to early man.

INDEX

Look out for other wacky books in this series... if you dare!

I finished reading this Truly Foul & Cheesy book on:

........../........../..........